Adapted and published in the United States
in 1986 by Silver Burdett Company,
Morristown, New Jersey

A TEMPLAR BOOK
Devised and produced by Templar Publishing Ltd,
Old King's Head Court, Dorking, Surrey RH4 1AR.

Library of Congress Cataloging-in-Publication Data
Stidworthy, John, 1943–
  Life begins.

  (Creatures from the past)
  Summary: Explains what the fossilized remains of
prehistoric animals have revealed about early life,
from the first sea creatures to the emergence of
reptiles.
  1. Paleontology—Juvenile literature
[1. Paleontology. 2. Fossils. 3. Prehistoric animals]
I. Parker, Steve. II. Forsey, Christopher, i11.
III. Title.
QE765.S75 1986   560   86-60988
ISBN 0-382-09320-8

Series editor: A J Wood
Editor: Nicholas Bellenberg
Designer: Mike Jolley
Production: Sandra Bennigsen

Origination: Anglia Reproductions, Witham, Essex
Printing: Purnell (Book Production) Ltd, Paulton, Bristol,
          Member of BPCC plc

PICTURE CREDITS
Page 8: Sinclair Stammers/Science Photo Library
Page 8-9: J.M. Start/ Robert Harding Picture Library
Page 9: (inset) David Bayliss/RIDA Photo Library
Page 12-13: Simon Conway-Morris/Sidgwick Museum

CREATURES FROM THE PAST

LIFE BEGINS

Written by
JOHN STIDWORTHY
MA (Cambridge)

Consultant Editor
STEVE PARKER
BSc Zoology

Illustrated by
CHRIS FORSEY

SILVER BURDETT COMPANY

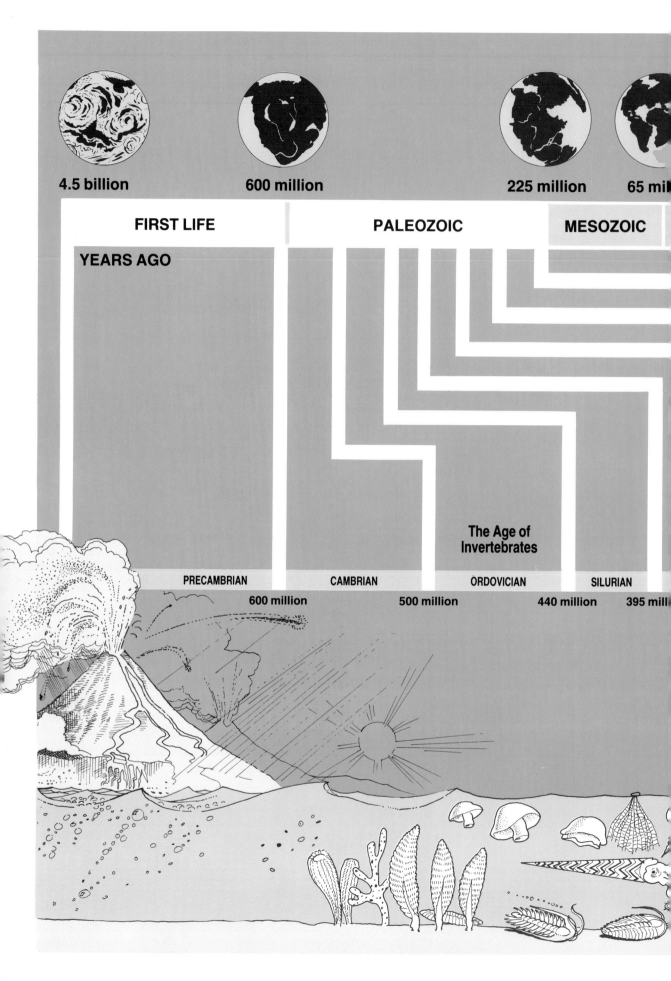

4.5 billion

600 million

225 million

65 mi

FIRST LIFE

PALEOZOIC

MESOZOIC

YEARS AGO

The Age of
Invertebrates

PRECAMBRIAN	CAMBRIAN	ORDOVICIAN	SILURIAN
600 million	500 million	440 million	395 milli

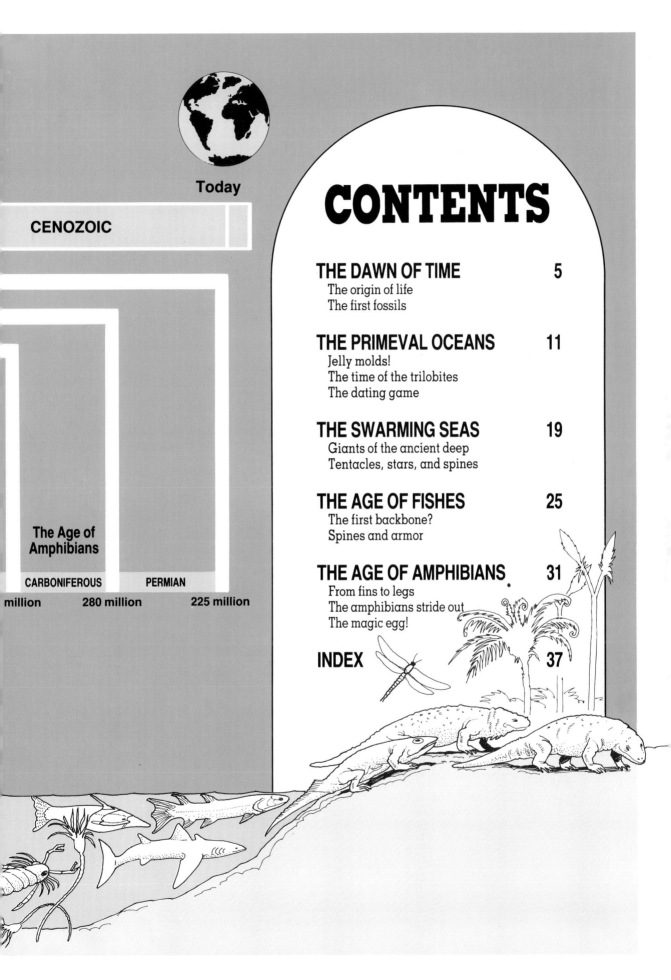

Today

CENOZOIC

The Age of
Amphibians

CARBONIFEROUS   PERMIAN

million   280 million   225 million

CONTENTS

THE DAWN OF TIME

The universe is vast beyond imagination. Planet Earth seems big to us, but it is quite small compared to some of the other eight planets that circle the Sun – our own star. The Sun is only one of the 100 billion or so stars in the Milky Way – our galaxy. And the Milky Way is only one of the 100 million or so galaxies that we know exist in the universe.

All the galaxies are flying away from each other through space, like debris from an explosion. So it is likely that at some time they were all together in one place and that there was a "big bang", which scattered all the matter in the universe. Scientists have calculated that this happened about 15 billion years ago, and, in a sense, this was the beginning of time.

After the bang, some of the matter began to collect under the force of gravity, forming clouds of gas which became the galaxies. This process continued in each galaxy, gradually forming the stars. Debris from around the stars, in turn, came together to create planets.

About 6 billion years ago, our Earth began to form when gases, dust, pieces of rock and metal came together under gravity. These melted and then the lighter rocks near the surface gradually cooled and became solid, forming the Earth's crust.

The age of some rocks can be measured quite accurately, and the oldest found on Earth date from 3.8 billion years ago. This, then, is the approximate age of our planet, the stage on which life was to appear...

The origin of life

For millions of years the early Earth was boiling hot, with giant volcanoes erupting and throwing rock, dust, and gases into the air. Electric storms flashed across the jagged new mountains and, as the atmosphere gradually cooled, rain lashed down on the rocks in storms that lasted for thousands of years. Nothing could live upon our planet.

The air of the early Earth contained no oxygen, which all animals and plants need to breathe to stay alive. But there were other gases in the atmosphere given off by the volcanoes, including nitrogen, ammonia, methane, water vapor, and perhaps carbon monoxide and carbon dioxide. Most of these gases are poisonous to living things, so even after hundreds of millions of years, the Earth was not a very likely place for living things to appear.

Gradually, though, chemicals such as sugars and amino acids – which are found in living things today – began to build up in the seas and lakes. Nowadays, any sugars and other organic substances (those found in living things) floating in the sea would not last for long. They would be changed by the action of oxygen, used by animals, or absorbed by plants. Of course on the early Earth there was little oxygen, and no animals or plants, so these organic substances accumulated in the warm water until they made an "organic soup."

The chemicals in the soup then began to combine and change each other, producing different and more complex substances. Eventually, one with a special property formed – it could make copies of itself, which is one of the abilities that all living things possess. The substance that can do this is a long, curly, spring-shaped molecule called deoxyribonucleic acid (usually shortened to DNA).

Sometimes the copying process went a little wrong – enough to make the "copy" slightly different from the original. When this happened nature could begin to "choose" between the different versions. Life and the process of evolution had begun.

What is DNA?
DNA is made of two long, curly molecules coiled together. When these two molecules separate, each makes a copy of itself, to give two new molecules – the process of reproduction.

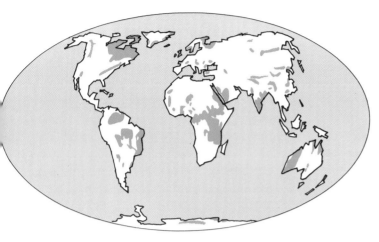

= Precambrian rock formations, about 3.8 billion years old.

How old are the rocks?

The age of the Earth's oldest rocks, from around the time when life began, in the Precambrian period, can actually be calculated. Some rocks contain small amounts of substances that are "radioactive," such as uranium 238. Over a period of time, this becomes less radioactive and change to lead. (You can read more about this on page 16.)

It is a slow process – it takes 4.5 billion years for half the uranium 238 in a rock to change into lead. Knowing this, scientists can carefully measure the amount of lead compared to the amount of uranium in a rock, and then work out how long ago it was formed. The oldest rocks on Earth have been found in Scotland, Canada, Africa, and Australia. They are about 3.8 billion years old.

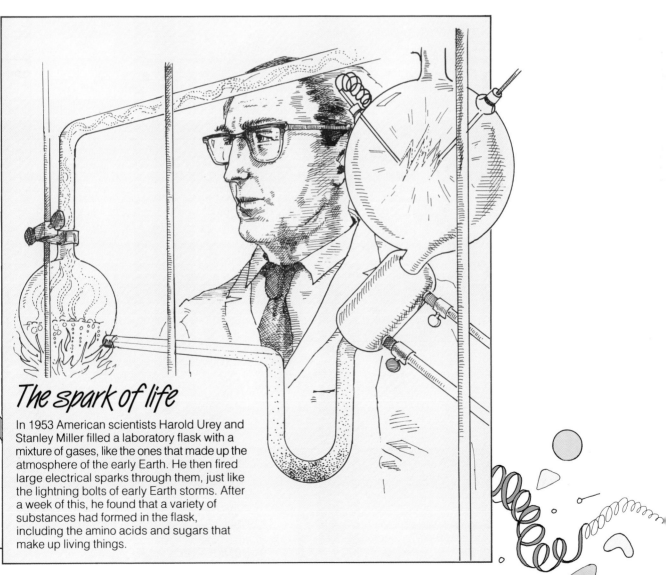

The spark of life

In 1953 American scientists Harold Urey and Stanley Miller filled a laboratory flask with a mixture of gases, like the ones that made up the atmosphere of the early Earth. He then fired large electrical sparks through them, just like the lightning bolts of early Earth storms. After a week of this, he found that a variety of substances had formed in the flask, including the amino acids and sugars that make up living things.

The first fossils

Fossils are the remains of plants and animals that have turned to stone. Until quite recently, it was believed that the oldest fossils were in rocks formed about 600 million years ago. But now we know that life goes back at least 3 billion years, to the time we call the Precambrian era, when the Earth was young. In fact, there have been living things for most of the time that our planet has existed. Scientists examining very old rocks have discovered the earliest signs of life – fossils which have been preserved against all the odds for many billions of years.

The first clue was the finding of *stromatolites* in the rocks. Stromatolites are rings, one inside the other, up to 3 feet across within the rock. Scientists wondered if they were made by a living creature, rather than simply being an odd formation in the rock.

Stromatolites in rocks from Lake Superior, in Canada, were the first to be thoroughly examined. Using special

Stromatolites today

Stromatolites can be seen growing today in a few special areas, such as lagoons in Australia's Great Barrier Reef (picture, right). Blue-green algae extract the chemical lime, which is dissolved in the water, and turn it into solid stone columns. Slices of these columns, like that in the right-hand circle above, show the stromatolite-like rings seen in the oldest rocks. The left-hand circle above shows a highly magnified slice through a fossil stromatolite. You can make out the shapes of bacteria and algae – the oldest fossils known.

saws, scientists cut slices of the stromatolite-containing rock (a flint called chert), and then ground them so thin that light could shine through them. They could then be looked at through a microscope. The great surprise was that traces of living things could be seen – mostly outlines of what seemed to be cell walls. It was possible to see bacteria, primitive plant-like growths known as blue-green algae, and other remains less easy to recognize. So it appeared that stromatolites were indeed made by living things – they were in fact the first fossils.

The first cherts investigated were "only" 1.9 billion years old. Soon other rocks, 3 billion years old, were studied and they contained these "microfossils" too. Even older stromatolites are known from Australia, showing that blue-green algae were alive before this time. And some chert 3 billion years old, from Greenland, has mysterious microscopic spheres inside it. These, too, could be the remains of some form of life – in which case they are the oldest fossils on our planet!

Small and simple

Blue-green algae (below) and bacteria (bottom) still thrive today and are the simplest living things. Each one is a single cell. It is made up of a skin or membrane surrounding a watery "soup" which contains all the molecules the cell needs to live, grow, feed and reproduce. It has no complicated internal parts like a nucleus, which plant and animal cells contain.

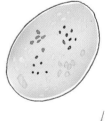

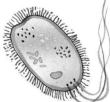

THE PRIMEVAL OCEANS

We can imagine what the teeming life in the primeval oceans was like, because of some extraordinary remains discovered in the rocks of the Ediacara hills, in southern Australia.

Today these rocks are hard sandstones, but 650 million years ago they were a soft, sandy beach on the edge of a sea. The dead bodies of sea creatures were washed up onto the beach and baked by the hot sun. Then, as the tide came in, they were buried by more sand. Their fossilized shapes survived as the sand was buried deeper and deeper and compressed into hard sandstone. Earth movements have tilted these rocks, wind and water have worn them away, and now the fossils lie on the surface.

All the creatures found at Ediacara were soft-bodied – that means they had no shells or bones or other hard parts. Their preservation in the fine-grained sandstone is almost a miracle for such soft creatures in such old rocks (you can read more about this on the next page). Although they are small, simple creatures compared to modern animals, they are much more complicated than earlier fossils. Many millions of years of evolution had to take place before animal life developed from the early bacteria to the jellyfish creatures of Ediacara. But we must wait until someone discovers fossils from the gap in between bacteria and jellyfish before we can know exactly what happened during this time.

How to say...

Spriggina
Sprig-een-a

Dickinsonia
Dick-in-sone-eea

Ediacara
Ed-ee-a-ka-ra

Foraminiferans
Fore-a-min-if-er-ans

Coccolith
Cock-o-lith

Ostracod
Ostra-kod

Jelly molds!

It takes very special conditions for soft-bodied creatures to become fossilized. Usually, only the hard parts, such as bones, shells, and teeth, are preserved as fossils. At Ediacara, which is shown on the previous page, there were special conditions. A beach with dead, sun-dried animals on it was quickly covered by fine sand. The finer the covering, the better the chance of small details being preserved.

Some of the finest fossils that scientists have ever found came from the Burgess Pass, in the Rocky Mountains of Canada. They were formed on the sea bed about 530 million years ago, in the middle of the geological period called the Cambrian. They are fossils of soft-bodied animals, and the special conditions allowed their jelly-like bodies to be molded in solid rock.

All those years ago the area was probably a deep, calm valley on the seabed. Towering above this submarine valley was an undersea mountain of soft, slippery silt. Sometimes there were massive avalanches on the mountain and a mixture of silt and water crashed into the valley below, engulfing some of the living creatures from above and burying them deeply. More and more silt piled up over the years, until eventually it hardened into solid rock, and the trapped animals were fossilized.

Because these animals were buried so quickly, perhaps in seconds, and by such fine silt, we can see incredible details in the fossils. Bristles, feathery gills, sometimes even muscles and intestines can be clearly seen. The conditions for preservation were so good that some of the animals found have never been seen anywhere else, before or since.

South Australia towards the end of the Precambrian

1 Jellyfishes *of many kinds pulsated through the seas. These "underwater umbrellas" were much like the modern jellyfish.*

2 Spriggina *and other weird worms crawled along the bottom or swam with the help of paddle-like flaps on their bodies.*

3 Dickinsonia *was a rounded worm which may have wriggled along like a snake.*

4 Sea pens *are coral-like animals, which form colonies shaped like old-fashioned quill pens stuck in the sea bed. Their fossils have been found in ancient rocks in central England as well as at Ediacara. Close relatives of these creatures still occur today.*

Common fossils

We tend to think of fossils as being rare finds. This is true for many groups, but there are some creatures and plants which were so common that whole layers of the Earth's rocks are made up of their remains. Three of these common groups are foraminiferans, coccoliths, and ostracods, shown below.

These and other "microfossils" in the rocks can be of great value to humans. Oil scientists know that particular microfossils occur in layers of rock which are often found above or below oil-bearing rocks. So the microfossils can be a helpful sign when test-drilling for new oilfields.

Foraminiferans

Foraminiferans are mostly microscopic single-celled animals, but they have hard shells with complicated patterns. Some limestone rocks are made up mainly of their skeletons. Foraminiferans are known from the Cambrian period onward.

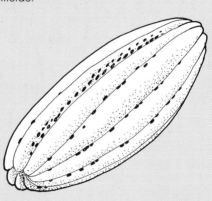

Coccoliths

The coccoliths are also "rock-makers." They are single-celled algae (plants) which have a shell made up of rings of lime crystals. When they die, the tiny rings fall to the bottom of the sea and gradually build up into limestone. They have helped to build many rocks, like the thick layers of chalk found in the Downs of southern England.

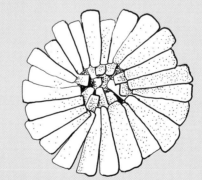

Ostracods

Ostracods appear in many rocks. These are relatives of shrimps, but look more like shellfish because their bodies are protected by a shell with two sides. Ostracods have been around for 450 million years. Most were tiny, but they were so numerous that when they died their tough little shells sank and made thick layers of rock on the sea bed.

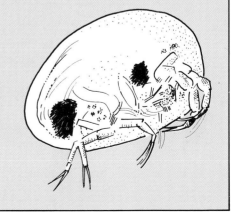

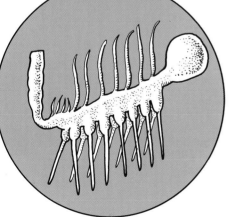

Can you believe it?

This strange creature was found among the Burgess Pass fossils. Called *Hallucigenia*, probably because the scientist who discovered it couldn't believe his eyes, it had seven pairs of legs, each pair with a tentacle above it. This animal is so odd that scientists have little idea to which present-day group it is related.

The time of the trilobites

One of the mysteries of life through the ages is when a successful group of animals, after flourishing for millions of years, becomes extinct. Scientists usually say that newer, more efficient animals evolved to replace them. But often it is not known why the newer group was better, or what was wrong with the old one! Sometimes we cannot even tell which animals *did* take over. A good example of such a mystery is the trilobite of the ancient seas.

The trilobites were one of the first big success stories of animal evolution. These creatures were divided into three along their length, a fact which gave them their name ("tri-lob-ite" meaning "three-lobed"). Their bodies were made up of segments, and each segment had a pair of jointed legs, similar to shrimps' legs. At the front was a head with a pair of eyes on top, and at the back a tail.

Like crabs and insects, the trilobites had a hard outer body shell which gave

protection to the softer parts inside. This skeleton was shed or moulted from time to time, so that the trilobite could grow. Many trilobite fossils are in fact fossils of these empty shells rather than of the whole animal. The fossils show the whole life-history of some species of trilobite, with up to 30 moults taking place between the tiny young larva and the fully-developed adult.

Many trilobites had legs around their mouths, which may have acted as "jaws." These would not have been very powerful though, so it is unlikely that they could catch and chew up large prey. Most probably they fed by scavenging on the sea bottom for small bits of plant and animal remains.

Trilobites were common in the Cambrian period (from 600 to 500 million years ago). They reached their greatest development shortly after, and then gradually declined. During their heyday at least 2,500 different kinds swam and crawled in the seas. But by about 225 million years ago all of them had become extinct.

Giant trilobite
Paradoxides *was one of the biggest trilobites measuring about 2 feet long. It lived about 550 million years ago.*

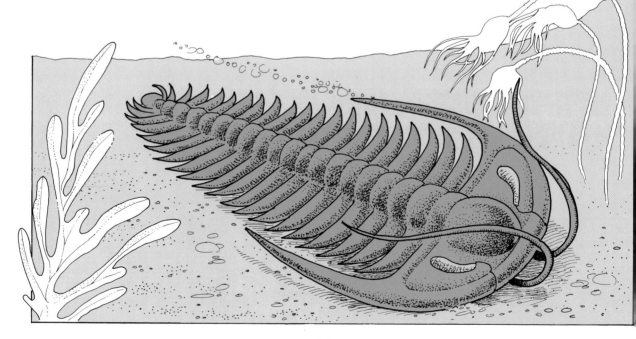

Seeing in the sea

Like its distant relatives, the insects, a trilobite had "compound" eyes. This means each eye was made up of many individual flat sections, called *facets*, like a cut diamond. Each facet received light from only one direction. The whole eye then built up an overall picture of the surroundings by combining all the individual pictures from each facet.

The fossil trilobite on the right, a species of *Calymene* found in Czechoslovakian pyrite rock 500 million years old, has large prominent eyes. We can guess from this that trilobites must have lived mainly in shallow, calm seas. Deep water would not have been light enough to see in, and neither would stirred-up muddy water, so their eyes would have been useless.

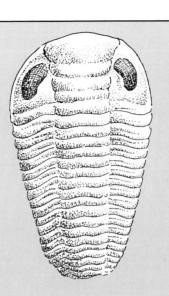

Smooth or spiny?

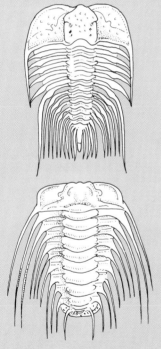

Two of the spiniest trilobites ever found are shown on the left. They are *Selenopeltis* (above) and *Cybeloides* (below) from the Ordovician period. Exactly why some trilobites had such long spikes all over them while others were quite smooth, is not clear. One theory is that the spines were useful for self-defense, since any predator trying to eat a spiny trilobite would get a prickly mouthful!

Trilobite armor

Smooth trilobites were protected against enemies by their tough skins, and perhaps some species burrowed into the soft sea bed so that they couldn't be turned over to expose their soft, vulnerable underparts. Others could curl up, like a woodlouse or hedgehog. One of these was *Calymene*. A lot of *Calymene* fossils have been found in a quarry at Dudley, near Birmingham, England. It was nicknamed the "Dudley bug," and many remains show it curled up. They must have reacted to danger or bad conditions, then died in this position.

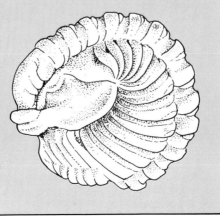

What became of the trilobites?

Trilobites seemed to be well adapted to their way of life, but died out as other animals evolved. We do not know the exact reason why, but they may have gradually been edged out by a whole range of competitors and predators.

The dating game

We know that the first living things appeared over 3 billion years ago... We know that trilobites died out around 225 million years ago... But how do we *know* these dates? How can we tell when an animal or plant lived, just from its fossil?

In fact, there are various methods of *dating* a fossil – that is, using various clues to work out roughly how old it is. One method of detection is to look at the type of rock the fossil is embedded in, and at any other fossils preserved with it. Another way is to make measurements of what is called the *radioactivity* of the fossil or its rock, as explained on the right.

Because of the way fossils are made (page 12), they are usually found in sedimentary rocks. These rocks are formed in horizontal layers, one above the other, with the oldest layer at the bottom and the youngest at the top. It follows then that any fossils found in the lower layers must be older than those in the upper layers.

Looking closer, we find that each rock layer contains its own particular mixture of fossils. The mixtures change from

Dating indicators

Graptolites (top) and brachiopods (bottom right) are important "index" fossils for dating. Graptolites are from the Ordovician and Silurian periods (500 to 395 million years ago). Brachiopods were very successful up to about 200 million years ago. The evolutionary changes in the distinctive shapes of these two creatures mean that they can be easily recognized and accurately dated.

Radioactive dating

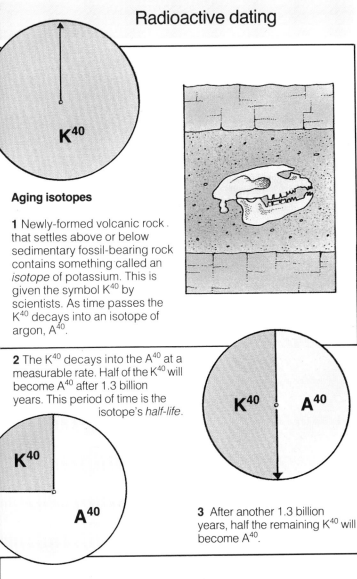

Aging isotopes

1 Newly-formed volcanic rock that settles above or below sedimentary fossil-bearing rock contains something called an *isotope* of potassium. This is given the symbol K^{40} by scientists. As time passes the K^{40} decays into an isotope of argon, A^{40}.

2 The K^{40} decays into the A^{40} at a measurable rate. Half of the K^{40} will become A^{40} after 1.3 billion years. This period of time is the isotope's *half-life*.

3 After another 1.3 billion years, half the remaining K^{40} will become A^{40}.

4 When fossils are discovered, samples of volcanic rock from nearby can be analyzed in a laboratory to work out how much A^{40} and K^{40} they contain. When the proportions of these isotopes are known, the age of the fossil can be deduced.

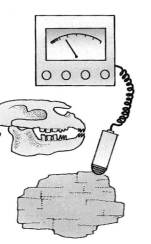

Other substances besides potassium are also used in these *radioactive* measurements, and they all have different half-lives. Radioactive dating methods allow scientists to carry out *absolute* dating, and the results are very accurate.

one layer to another because, as time passed, some animals became extinct while new ones evolved. The fossil mixtures also vary according to where in the world the rock layers formed, and whether it was a freshwater area or one covered in shallow seas or deep oceans. However, we have to be careful. The movements of the Earth's crust could have lifted layers, tilted them at crazy angles, or even turned them right over, and all this must be taken into account in the investigation.

The most useful fossils that make up the characteristic mixtures are of small, plentiful animals that had easily-preserved shells or other hard parts. Animals like this include mollusks (relatives of snails) and the ostracods and foraminiferans shown on page 13. Trilobites are helpful for the Cambrian period. Plant fossils are useful, too. Grains of pollen and seeds are plentiful and easily preserved and, like animal remains, they are found in characteristic mixtures which make extremely useful time markers.

So far, so good. We know how old one fossil is, relative to another. But can we give them real, *absolute* dates? The answer to this question is "Yes," and we do it partly by finding out how fast sedimentary rocks are formed today. Then, assuming that rocks were made at the same rate in the past, we can travel back in time by digging down into the Earth. If a fossil is buried a certain number of feet down, then we can work out roughly that it must have been trapped there so many millions of years ago.

But again, we have to be careful. Different types of sedimentary rock form at different speeds in different conditions. Also, we must remember that layers of rock which formed on top of the fossil may have been worn away in more recent times, giving us a false idea of how deep the remains really are.

THE SWARMING SEAS

In the Ordovician period, from 500 to 440 million years ago, the seas were filled with all manner of strange new animals. The first starfishes, sea urchins, and other echinoderms (spiny-skins) evolved. Early corals, helped by bryozoans (sea mats), built limestone reefs in the warm, shallow waters. These tiny animals lived together in colonies, each making a hard limestone skeleton.

The colonies varied greatly in size and shape between species. Some were flattened, others were upright, some were rounded and lumpy while others were thin and branching. The shapes of these animals and their reefs give us valuable evidence when dating the less common fish and other creatures preserved with them.

Other creatures, which had already evolved before this time, increased their success. The trilobites were at their most numerous. There were all shapes and sizes of brachiopods, which are also called lamp shells. The nautiloids, early relatives of the octopus, reached their greatest size. And water-living eurypterids, or sea scorpions, stalked the seabed and preyed on other animals.

This was truly the Age of Invertebrates, for almost all these animals, big and small, lacked backbones. But a new group of animals was beginning to develop. Although they were small, rare and not yet very important, the first vertebrates (animals with backbones) had evolved. Soon things on the Earth would change forever.

How to say...

Lyssacina
Liss-a-seen-a

Chenendopora
Chen-en-dough-pore-a

Marrolithus
Marrow-lith-us

Opipeuter
Owe-pee-pewt-er

Scyphocrinites
Sky-foe-krin-eye-tees

Cheirocrinus
Keer-owe-krin-us

Eurypterus
Ewe-rip-tear-us

Giants of the ancient deep

The biggest animals of the Ordovician seas, some 450 million years ago, were the nautiloids. Some of these mollusks grew to over 13 feet long, with a straight shell narrowing to a point at one end and the creature's head at the other. In fact, a nautiloid looked somewhat like an octopus stuck in a multicolored ice cream cone!

Nautiloids belong to the mollusk family. Mollusks are invertebrates (which means they don't have backbones), usually characterized by their shells. However, there are exceptions – like today's squids and octopuses, which don't have shells, but are still mollusks!

The nautiloid had lots of tentacles around its mouth, all-seeing eyes, and was one of the swiftest sea dwellers of its time. Not all were large, but still they must have been fearsome predators. Nautiloids were very numerous for a while, but by about 380 million years ago they were beginning to die out. Only six species remain today, the relatives of octopuses, squids, and cuttlefish.

Sea scorpions were another group of giant predators, but are not very well named. For a start, not all of them lived in the sea – they did evolve in sea water but some moved to slightly salty or even fresh water. They weren't true scorpions either, although they did belong to the arachnids – the group that includes spiders and scorpions.

A typical sea scorpion, or eurypterid, had a long flat body made of segments. Its head had two large eyes, with two smaller "eye spots" between them, and underneath were its walking legs. In front of these were two strong pincers.

A eurypterid looks "multi-purpose." It could have swum, walked, or burrowed

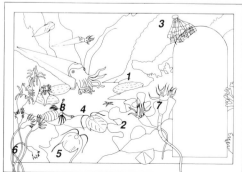

A shallow sea during the Ordovician period

1 Lyssacina, *and* **2** Chenendopora, *were sponges – very simple animals made of cells with tiny spiky pieces of silica for a skeleton.*

3 Dictyonema *was a net-shaped graptolite (page 16) about 4 inches long.*

4 Marrolithus, *and* **5** Opipeuter, *were trilobites of the time, less than an inch long.*

6 Scyphocrinites *was a beautiful sea-lily – not a plant, but an echinoderm. Its tentacles swept the water for tiny plant and animal food.*

7 Cheirocrinus *was a cystoid, an extinct type of echinoderm. Its waving tentacles collected food and its hollow body was held to the seabed by a stalk.*

8 Eurypterus *was a sea scorpion.*

Nautiloid in hiding
Orthoceras *lived about 410 million years ago. It could retreat into its shell and close it with a hard "door" when danger threatened. It was about 1 yard long.*

n mud. But its main advantage was its
ize. Even the smaller sea scorpions
vere large compared to the creatures
hey hunted, while the largest grew to
early 10 feet long! Lying in wait near
he sea bed, and grabbing prey when it
ame near enough, they were the
igers of the ocean before they
inally became
extinct.

Feeling the pinch!
Pterygotus *hunted in the seas about 400 million years ago. Its body was 6 feet long. Few animals (like the fish above) could have escaped from its terrible pincers.*

Tentacles, stars, and spines

Many creatures, besides those on the previous pages, became common and then died out during the Age of Invertebrates.

Most of these animals had soft, fleshy bodies and no skeletons. Usually only hard parts like shells are preserved as fossils, but sometimes we are lucky. Some beautifully preserved belemnite fossils have been discovered in Bavaria, Germany. These show all the soft parts of the animal in great detail, and were formed by the same kind of "lucky accident" that made the fossils of Ediacara and Burgess Pass.

Even if only fossil shells are found, paleontologists can deduce what the rest of the animal looked like, by comparing the shell to that of a living relative. Fossil ammonite shells are very common, and very similar to the shell of *Nautilus*, a present-day nautiloid with a curved shell. Looking at the way *Nautilus's* body works, we can guess how ammonites might have moved.

In an empty *Nautilus* shell, you can see a line where a very thin part of the animal's body was partly embedded in the inside of the shell. The living *Nautilus* uses this part of its body to vary the amount of air that it keeps in its shell. If it pumps in more air, then the animal will be lighter in water and will rise nearer the surface. Absorbing some air from the shell will mean that the animal gets heavier in the water and will sink nearer to the bottom.

Fossil ammonite shells have a line in them, just like the *Nautilus* shell of today. This similarity means that an ammonite could probably rise and sink in a similar way to *Nautilus*. But we can only guess what the ammonites ate and what their soft parts looked like.

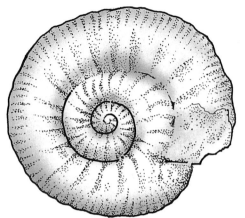

Fossil ammonite

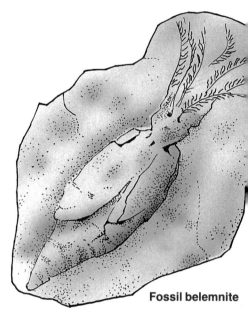

Fossil belemnite

Mollusk relatives

Ammonites and belemnites (living examples of which are shown on the right) were the relations of present-day mollusks – snails, squids, and octopuses. They were common from 200 million to 65 million years ago. Ammonites evolved from the nautiloids and were very varied. Some were only the size of a coin, while others grew up to 6 feet across. They evolved very quickly, and are good dating "labels."

Belemnite fossils are usually of the creature's strong bullet-shaped shell. The whole creature was like a squid and probably swam backwards, trailing its tentacles behind it. The tentacles had rows of little hooks to catch prey, and inside its body the belemnite had an ink sac. It used to squirt out the ink to make a "smoke screen" in the water when it was in danger – just like a modern squid does

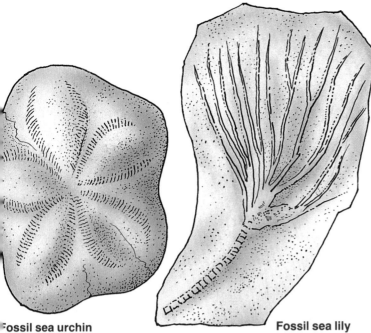

Sea urchins and sea lilies

Sea urchins and sea lilies (seen in their living form below) are members of the echinoderm group, dating from Ordovician times. Some sea urchins are beautifully preserved as fossils, and early ones had thin shells made up of little plates like roof tiles. Both fossil and modern sea urchins have tiny "tube feet" which emerge from small holes in their shells. These feet are special to echinoderms. They are finger-shaped, fluid-filled bags, which can be pumped up and let down for walking, grasping and feeling.

Sea lilies are not plants, but members of the crinoid family of echinoderms. They were actually known as fossils long before their living relatives were discovered in the depths of the oceans.

Fossil sea urchin

Fossil sea lily

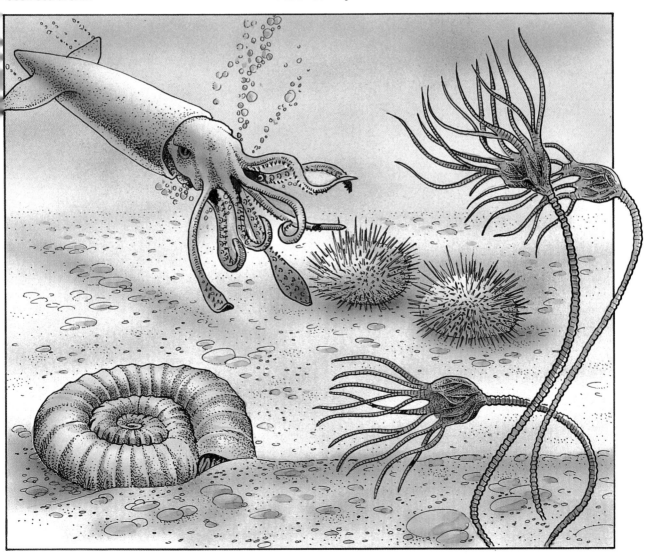

THE AGE OF FISHES

During the Devonian period, from 395 to 345 million years ago, there was an explosion in evolution. The first backboned animals, the fishes, appeared in enormous numbers and variety. They evolved first in the seas and soon made their way into freshwater rivers and lakes.

Many of the early vertebrates were not true fishes. They had backbones and they swam, but they had no jaws and lacked the paired fins found in real fishes. Even so, all the main groups of fishes living today began in the Devonian.

Things were beginning to happen on land, too. Several types of spore-bearing plants began to flourish there, such as horsetails, clubmosses, and ferns. Some of these began to grow quite large, forming the first forests. With plants as a food source it was not long before the first land animals evolved. Insects were at the forefront of the land invasion, closely followed by the first amphibians (as you can read on page 31).

Meanwhile, back in the water the true jawed, finned fishes soon took over from the jawless versions. Some stayed small and insignificant; some evolved armor-plating to protect themselves from others who became the giant hunters of the Devonian deep, larger than the biggest sharks of today. Some, such as the placoderms, flourished briefly but quickly became extinct. By the end of the Devonian one group of fishes had moved on to yet another adventure – they had gained a finhold on the land!

How to say...

Dinichthys
Die-nik-thiss

Chirodipterus
Kye-row-dip-tur-us

Pteraspis
Tear-as-piss

Birkenia
Burk-een-ee-a

Lungmenshanaspis
Lung-men-shan-as-piz

Climatius
Kly-mate-ee-us

Acanthodes
Ack-an-thow-dees

The first backbone?

One of the greatest advances in evolution was the development of the backbone. Fishes, amphibians, reptiles, birds, and mammals – including humans of course – all have a backbone, or spine. When did this amazing feature evolve, and why was it so successful?

It is not known for certain which animal was the ancestor of the vertebrates (animals with backbones) but this is not really surprising. We are not sure what kind of creature we are looking for in the fossil record, or even whether it would have been fossilized at all since it might have been soft-bodied.

There is, however, one living creature that could tell us what the vertebrate ancestor may have looked like. This is a small eel-like animal called *Amphioxus*, otherwise known as the lancelet. It lives in the sea, usually with its body buried in sand and its head sticking out. It sucks water in through its mouth, filters out food particles, then pushes out the remaining water through its gill slits.

Instead of a backbone, this little creature has a pencil-like rod of strong tissue running down its back, called a notochord. Its main nerve cord runs just above. In vertebrates, the nerves are grouped together in a similar cord that runs up the spine to the creature's brain. So you can see why scientists believe that the notochord was the forerunner of the backbone. In fact, the young of backboned animals still pass through a stage with a notochord as they develop.

The importance of this rod (whether it's a notochord or a true backbone) is that it helps to stiffen and support the body, and it provides somewhere for the rows of muscles along the body to attach, so that they work efficiently. Animals like *Amphioxus* have been found in the Burgess shale rocks of 550 million years ago. This basic design for backboned animals has remained similar ever since, although the number of improvements has been enormous.

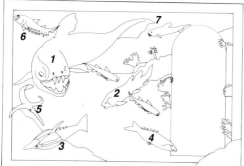

The warm waters of the Devonian

1 Dinichthys *was an arthrodire nearly 35 feet long. It was the largest animal of the time.*

2 Chirodipterus, *an early type of lungfish, looked similar to its relatives today.*

3 Pteraspis *(8 inches long), had no true fins. It was probably a clumsy swimmer.*

4 Birkenia *belonged to the anaspids, which like the ostracoderms, had no jaws or true fins.*

5 Lungmenshanaspis *(10 inches in length) was a galeaspid, similar to an ostracoderm.*

6 Climatius *belonged to the acanthodians. Though shown here in the sea, it probably lived in fresh water.*

7 Acanthodes *was another acanthodian, one of the last survivors before the group died out around 260 million years ago.*

From gills to jaws

Gills allowed the next big leap forward in vertebrate design. Gills are the parts of a water-dwelling animal which absorb oxygen from the water, allowing the creature to "breathe." Gills were supported by bony bars in the first creatures to have them. But as evolution continued, the bars nearest the mouth changed their job and position, bending around the mouth to form an upper and lower jaw. The skin in this area grew bony scales which were much bigger and sharper than ordinary body scales. These developed to become teeth. The fish, as it had now become, was able to bite and chew larger lumps of food, and even catch large animals.

This was a great advance. Jaws meant that many more ways of life were possible, instead of just filter-feeding or sucking up tiny food particles from the sea bed. The fishes evolved rapidly to take advantage of these new evolutionary "inventions" and soon the seas swarmed with jawed, finned vertebrates.

■ = Bones
■ = Gill slits

Useful gills
1 In a primitive ostracoderm there is a row of gills, each one the same and supported by a bony bar.

2 In a more advanced fish, an acanthodian, the first gill bars have become bony plates in the eye socket. The second gill bars have bent forward to form the jaws.

3 In an even more advanced fish, a fossil shark, the third gill bars have become part of the hearing organ. What were the fourth gill bars are now the first!

Notochord history

Amphioxus is an insignificant little creature only 2 inches long which lives a quiet life in the sandy bed of warm, shallow seas. There are about 25 different species of *Amphioxus* around the world. Each one has a notochord – an early version of the backbone, which makes this animal an important link in evolutionary history. Scientists are not sure whether it belongs in the vertebrate or invertebrate groups. Most include it in an in-between group called the Cephalochordata!

Spines and armor

As the Age of Fishes continued, various groups evolved and died out. The ostracoderms, anaspids, galeaspids, and acanthodians (all mentioned on the previous pages) eventually disappeared. So did the placoderms, yet another group of armor-plated fish. But in the middle of the Devonian period, 370 million years ago, placoderms ruled the seas.

Some placoderms, like *Pterichthyodes*, were quite small. This type had a strange bony armor, which went not just over its head and body, but down its front fins too. Scientists believe that this fish crawled along the sea bed using its fins as stilts or "legs," because some of the fossils show signs of wear on the ends of the fin covers.

The largest placoderms are called arthrodires. These had strong shields on their heads, hinged to equally strong plates on their chests. At the back end some species had scales, although later arthrodires had bare skin near the tail. *Coccosteus* is a well-known fossil arthrodire.

On fossil arthrodires of all shapes and sizes there are grooves in the armor plating running along the body. These probably contained the sensitive "lateral line" that fishes have today. It helps them "feel" water currents and other animals' movements. So this useful feature evolved very early on in vertebrate history.

The arthrodires reached their peak late in the Devonian period, in terms of both numbers and size. In fact, some became bigger than any previous animal, and bigger than most fishes since. The biggest was the giant *Dinichthys* – nearly 35 feet long!

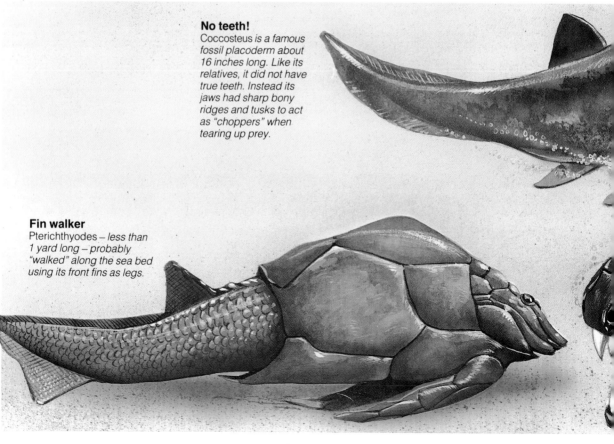

No teeth!
Coccosteus *is a famous fossil placoderm about 16 inches long. Like its relatives, it did not have true teeth. Instead its jaws had sharp bony ridges and tusks to act as "choppers" when tearing up prey.*

Fin walker
Pterichthyodes – *less than 1 yard long – probably "walked" along the sea bed using its front fins as legs.*

The successful shark

Sharks first appeared in the Devonian period. They are sometimes referred to as "primitive" fish, but that does not mean they are inefficient or badly designed. It just means that they evolved a long time ago. Although their descendants have changed in some ways, the same overall design is as successful now as it was nearly 400 million years ago.

Sharks' skeletons are not made from bone, but cartilage, which is quite soft and unlikely to fossilize. Most fossil sharks are known from their preserved teeth, but occasionally some whole fossil sharks are found. One such is the streamlined *Cladoselache*, from the late Devonian period, which was preserved in shale rock in America.

Modern shark

Cladoselache

Bone blades
Dinichthys was a fearsome giant of its time. Its huge mouth was armed with cutting blades of bone 24 inches high.

THE AGE OF AMPHIBIANS

The Carboniferous period, from 345 to 280 million years ago, is often called the Age of the Amphibians. Although fishes flourished in the seas and many plants and insects lived on the land, amphibians were the most advanced animals of this time and evolved quickly. They lived on land *and* in water. They laid their eggs in the water; the eggs hatched into swimming tadpoles; and as the tadpoles became adult they moved onto the land.

Huge steamy, swampy forests covered large areas of the Carboniferous world. These swamps provided ideal habitats for amphibians. The "trees" in these forests were actually giant horsetails and clubmosses, crawling with cockroaches, giant dragonflies, spiders and scorpions. So there was plenty of food for the amphibians as they crawled from the water.

Many early amphibians were shaped like their modern descendants, the newts – but some were more than 6 feet long, much larger than any amphibian alive today.

At the end of the Carboniferous, the Age of the Amphibians was nearly over. Many died out, a few stayed as they were, while others returned to the water full-time. The remainder were able to move permanently onto the land, because their eggs had developed shells and so they no longer needed to lay them in the water.

So the amphibians became reptiles – the creatures which were soon to dominate the world for hundreds of millions of years.

How to say...

Dolichosoma
Doll-itch-oh-so-ma

Eogyrinus
Eee-oh-gee-rine-us

Meganeura
Meg-an-new-rah

Discosauriscus
Disco-saw-iss-cus

Calamites
Cal-am-ite-ees

Sigillaria
Sig-ill-air-ee-ah

Psaronius
Sar-own-ee-us

From fins to legs

By the end of the Devonian period the bony fishes had evolved into two main groups. One was the "ray-fins." These went on to become very successful. Nearly all the 20,000 bony fish species living today are ray-fins.

The second group was the "lobe-fins." About 300 million years ago they were very numerous and successful. Today there are only a few species left. But they "live on" in another way, because their lobed fins gradually evolved into legs! All land animals with backbones – amphibians, reptiles, birds and mammals – are in fact descended from the primitive lobe-finned fish.

This evolutionary step may have happened because in the Devonian period some parts of the world seem to have had a changeable climate. Lakes and ponds must have filled up and dried out quite regularly. A fish with lobe fins might have been able to push itself across a mud-bank to a bigger pool, to escape when its own pool dried up. The ray fin, being much weaker and more flimsy, probably could not do the job as well.

The lobe-fins had another advantage over the ray-fins. Inside a fish's body is a hollow bag called a swim bladder. This contains air, to make the fish lighter so that it can swim more easily. In most ray-fins the swim bladder is not connected to the mouth. But in a lobe-fin it *is* connected to the mouth, by a tube in the throat. So the lobe-fin can gulp air into its swim bladder. When a Devonian pool dried up, this could come in useful as a temporary way of breathing. In fact, there are still some fish alive today – the lungfish – that do exactly this. It was the first step in the change from fish to amphibian, and it took place in the Devonian. As one pool dried out, lobe-finned fish could crawl to another one on their strong fins, gulping air as they went. *Eusthenopteron* and *Ichthyostega* are two fossil creatures which show us how the change probably took place.

A "living fossil?"
Coelacanths were a group of lobe-fins which were common from 370 million to 70 million years ago. After that time, they disappeared. But one species of coelacanth was rediscovered in 1938, living in the depths of the Indian Ocean. However, scientists do not believe that the modern coelacanth is a "living fossil," similar to the ancient coelacanths.

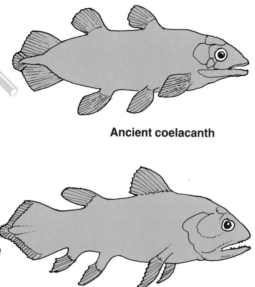

Ancient coelacanth

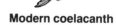

Modern coelacanth

Life in a Carboniferous swamp

1 Dolichosoma *was an early amphibian, though it looked like a snake. (Snakes had not yet evolved.)*

2 Eogyrinus *(10 feet long) was another amphibian that looked like a reptile – in this case, a crocodile.*

3 Giant insects *such as the dragonfly* Meganeura *and early cockroaches crawled and flew among the Carboniferous plants.*

4 Discosauriscus *was an amphibian 16 inches long.*

5 Calamites *– giant horsetails – grew up to 65 feet tall.*

6 Sigillaria *was a giant clubmoss, 50 feet high.*

7 *The tree fern* Psaronius *grew up to 27 feet tall. It is the ancient relative of some of today's ferns.*

Skin and bones

In a ray-finned fish (below), each fin has a narrow base. The main part of the fin is supported by thin fan-shaped rays, which are made of hardened skin.

In a lobe-finned fish (bottom), there is a solid lobe of flesh at the bottom of the fin. The main part of the fin is supported by bones within this. Skin rays are just on the outer part of the fin.

Eusthenopteron (the fish at the bottom) was a lobe-fin about 3 feet long. The bones in the lobe part of its fin were arranged with one long bone nearest the body, then two bones next to it, and a collection of smaller bones toward the outside. You can see this in the left hand circle. The bones inside a limb have a similar arrangement, and are shown in the right hand circle.

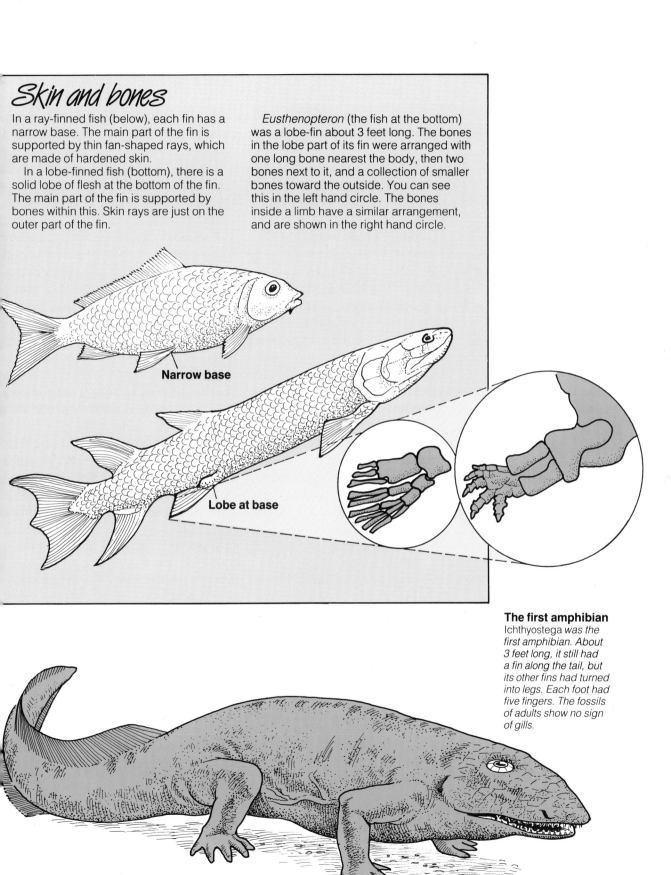

Narrow base

Lobe at base

The first amphibian
Ichthyostega *was the first amphibian. About 3 feet long, it still had a fin along the tail, but its other fins had turned into legs. Each foot had five fingers. The fossils of adults show no sign of gills.*

The amphibians stride out

When the amphibians moved onto land, life was easier in some ways. Food was abundant, and there were few other large creatures to fight with. But there were plenty of problems to overcome.

Air does not support an animal's body as well as water. Legs, hips, shoulders, and backbone needed strengthening to allow the amphibians to move easily in their new surroundings. *Eryops*, of about 260 million years ago, had strong legs and a powerful backbone to support its 6 foot long body on the land. But like other amphibians, its legs jutted out from the side of its body. This made it difficult to lift the body clear of the ground. (When the reptiles evolved, this was one of the problems they solved, by having their legs underneath their bodies.)

Living on land made seeing difficult, too. Fishes' eyes are constantly bathed in water and so are always clean and moist. In air, this sort of eye would dry up and get dirty. So eyelids evolved to protect the eyes – they were able to blink and wipe the surface of the eye clean. Special tear glands also developed to make tears which kept the eyes moist.

Hearing was another problem. Sound traveling through water also travels through the body of a fish. So ears deep in the fish's body can register the sound. But on land things are much different. Many sounds traveling through the air would simply bounce off an amphibian's body. To hear, it needs ears on its body's surface. So two thin areas of skin, the eardrums, evolved on the surface just behind the head. A small bone which was part of the jaw support in fishes (see page 27) became attached to this, to conduct sounds to the deeper part of the ear.

Despite these and other adaptations, by about 200 million years ago the giant amphibians had faded out. Their representatives today are frogs, toads, newts, salamanders, and a few burrowing, legless worm-like creatures called caecilians – small reminders of their huge relatives that once roamed the Earth.

Leather skin?
Eryops remains have been found mainly in America. Its skin was leathery, with only small scales and it probably fed in the water, catching smaller amphibians and fish.

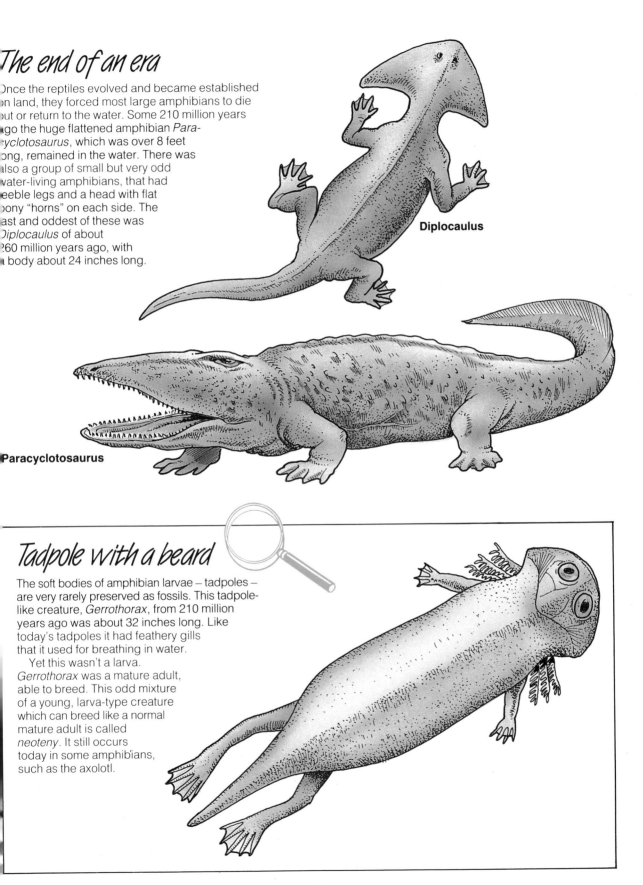

The end of an era

Once the reptiles evolved and became established on land, they forced most large amphibians to die out or return to the water. Some 210 million years ago the huge flattened amphibian *Paracyclotosaurus*, which was over 8 feet long, remained in the water. There was also a group of small but very odd water-living amphibians, that had feeble legs and a head with flat bony "horns" on each side. The last and oddest of these was *Diplocaulus* of about 260 million years ago, with a body about 24 inches long.

Diplocaulus

Paracyclotosaurus

Tadpole with a beard

The soft bodies of amphibian larvae – tadpoles – are very rarely preserved as fossils. This tadpole-like creature, *Gerrothorax*, from 210 million years ago was about 32 inches long. Like today's tadpoles it had feathery gills that it used for breathing in water.

Yet this wasn't a larva. *Gerrothorax* was a mature adult, able to breed. This odd mixture of a young, larva-type creature which can breed like a normal mature adult is called *neoteny*. It still occurs today in some amphibians, such as the axolotl.

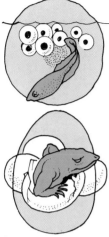

Soft or hard eggs?
The amphibian's egg had no shell. It had to be laid in water, where its young also lived. Both eggs and tadpoles were in great danger of being eaten.
The reptile's egg had a leathery or hard shell instead. It could be laid on dry land, hidden from predators.

The magic egg!

Although the Age of Amphibians lasted a long time – many tens of millions of years – the amphibians themselves could never leave the water behind. This was where they laid their eggs, and where their tadpoles grew up. Many adult amphibians had damp, slimy skins that needed to be kept moist by regular swims. They were mostly fish-eaters, and had the pointed teeth of their fishy ancestors. Even a late amphibian like *Eryops* still had the same type of teeth as the fish *Eusthenopteron*.

But some of the amphibians did evolve. They developed a waterproof skin so that they could move from damp areas to really dry places. And they evolved a waterproof egg that could be laid on land, in other words, they became reptiles.

Before the end of the Carboniferous period, 280 million years ago, the first reptiles had evolved from amphibians. We can work this out from fossil skeletons, even though the most important advances, the scaly skin and shelled egg, have not generally fossilized.

Besides the waterproof scaly skin and the shelled egg, early reptiles also found a new food source – land plants. These were much tougher than water plants, so the front teeth of some reptiles became chisel-shaped for cutting leaves, while the back teeth took on a flat shape for chewing.

Reptiles gradually took over from amphibians during the Permian and Triassic periods, up to 195 million years ago. From then on, dinosaurs and other giant reptiles ruled the world for millions of years. The Day of the Dinosaur had arrived...

Reptile or amphibian?

Seymouria lived about 260 million years ago. In almost every part of its body it was midway between an amphibian and a reptile. At one time it was thought to be the ancestor of all reptiles. Now scientists believe it was an amphibian with reptile-like features, on a side-branch of the main evolutionary tree.

INDEX